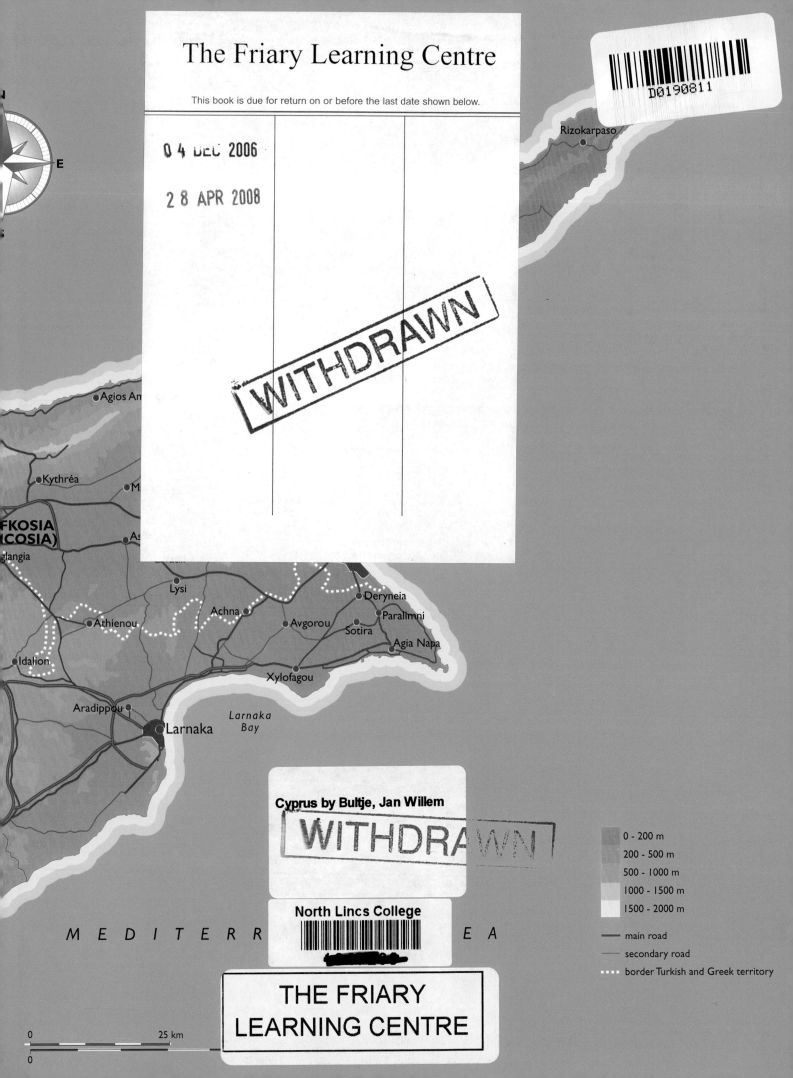

The Friary Learning Centre

This book is due for return on or before the last date shown below.

D0190811

Rizokarpaso

Agios An...

Kythréa

FKOSIA
(COSIA)
glangia

Lysi

Deryneia

Achna

Paralimni

Avgorou

Athienou

Sotira

Agia Napa

Idalion

Xylofagou

Aradippou

Larnaka

Larnaka
Bay

M E D I T E R R ... E A

0 - 200 m
200 - 500 m
500 - 1000 m
1000 - 1500 m
1500 - 2000 m

main road
secondary road
border Turkish and Greek territory

0

25 km

0

A Cherrytree Book

This edition published in 2006 by Evans Brothers Limited
2A Portman Mansions
Chiltern Street
London W1U 6NR, UK

Published by arrangement with KIT Publishers, The Netherlands

British Library Cataloguing-in-Publication Data
Bultje, Jan Willem
Cyprus. - (New EU countries and citizens)
1. Cyprus - Juvenile literature
I. Title
956.9'3
ISBN 1842343297
9781842343296

Text: Jan Willem Bultje
Photographs: Jan Willem Bultje
Translation: Arnoud Alting van Geusau
UK editing: Sonya Newland
Cover: Big Blu Ltd
Cartography: Armand Haye, Amsterdam, The Netherlands
Production: J & P Far East Productions, Soest, The Netherlands

Picture Credits

Photographs: Jan Willem Bultje
p. 26, 28 (t l), 35 (t), 36 (t r), 43, 37: EPA Photo, Katia Christodoulou;
p. 16(l) © James Davis; Eye Ubiquitous/CORBIS; p. 44 © Michael Gore; Frank Lane
Picture Agency/CORBIS; p.24 (t), 38: Cyprus Tourist Agency

Contents

Introduction

The island of Cyprus is steeped in history. It has been inhabited since the Stone Age, and because of its strategic position close to Asia, Europe and Africa, it has been subject to periods of invasion, conflict and foreign rule over the centuries.

Cyprus lies in the eastern Mediterranean Sea. On the mainland, around 80 km to the north, lies Turkey, 110 km to the east is Syria, and 350 km to the south is North Africa.

After many years of control by foreign nations, the island was granted independence in 1960. However, this did not bring about an end to its troubles. After more years of conflict, the two main groups on Cyprus – Greek Cypriots and Turkish Cypriots – divided the island into two parts in 1974. The northern part is Turkish and the southern part is Greek. Both of these languages are spoken on Cyprus, and English is also widely used. In fact, there are many British aspects of life on the island, as it was once a British colony.

Cyprus is too small in area to be divided into provinces. There are, however, six districts in the southern part. These are Famagusta, Kyrenia, Larnaca, Limassol, Nicosia and Paphos. The capital and largest city is Nicosia, and the border between north and south runs through the city.

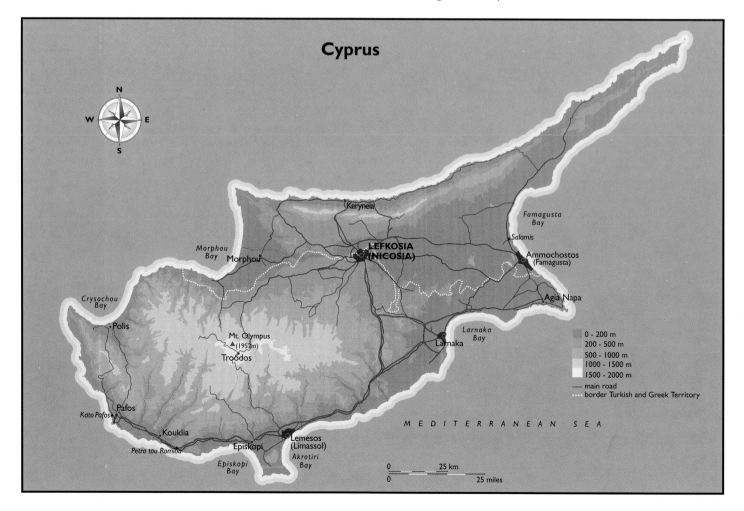

There is much on Cyprus to attract tourists and it is a popular holiday destination because of its warm climate and hundreds of historical sites. Most of these are remnants of the different peoples who have inhabited Cyprus over many centuries. They range from Stone Age huts to magnificent mosaics left behind by the Romans. Since that time, many other nations have settled on Cyprus, and hilltop forts built by the Crusader knights in the Middle Ages, small churches, mosques and castles that date from the fifteenth and sixteenth centuries can all be found scattered across the island.

Although tourism is important in both parts of the island, the economy also relies on other industries. Agriculture is a significant source of income in north and south. Fishing is a key industry in the Turkish sector, while the Greek sector has a strong manufacturing trade.

The division of the country means that it is a land of diverse cultures and traditions, from the style of the architecture to the religious practices of the Cypriot people.

▲ *In the Republic of Cyprus (the south of the country), the currency is the Cypriot pound. This is a one-pound note.*

▼ *There are many old buildings all over Cyprus. This is the Archangelos church, built in the twelfth century, in the village Káto Léfkara.*

History

Cyprus has been inhabited since the Stone Age. The earliest-known people to live there, around 5600 BC, were a race of farmers called the Choirokoiti. They were named after the village in which in they lived – Choirokoitia, which lies in the southern part of the island. The village was built on the side of a hill, and was surrounded by a thick stone wall, which acted as a defence against other tribes who might settle on the island. The people lived in round stone huts with flat roofs.

▼ Archeologists discovered that the Choirokoiti buried their dead beneath their huts. Remains were found during excavations of the site.

Kyprus

The transition from the Stone Age to the Bronze Age took place between 3900 and 2500 BC. Throughout this transition period, tools and weapons made from stone were slowly replaced by those made from copper. Cyprus was rich in copper and there was a great demand for this 'modern' metal. As a result, Cyprus became an important trading post. The island was named after the Greek word for copper, *kyprus*. The peak of the Copper Age on the island was between 2800 and 2500 BC.

▼ These replica buildings show the huts as they would have looked when the Choirokoiti lived in the village.

◀ The entrance to one of the royal graves. Openings like this were hewn into the rock so that the dead could be placed there.

▲ This chamber is part of the royal grave complex at Kato Paphos on Cyprus. Important people were buried here in ancient Greek and Roman times.

The development of trade with countries like Crete and Egypt brought great wealth to Cyprus. The pharaoh of Egypt even offered Cyprus the protection of his powerful armies in exchange for the metal. However, copper is quite a soft metal, so tools and weapons made from it were not very durable. People began to use a new metal, bronze, which is an alloy of copper and tin, and is much harder than pure copper. This discovery ushered in the Bronze Age (2500–1050 BC).

During this time, many people travelled from the Greek mainland to Cyprus, fleeing from natural disasters and war. It was a dangerous time for the inhabitants of the island, and they began to build walls and fortifications around several cities for protection. Many weapons and graves have been discovered dating from this period.

By the ninth century BC, most people living on the island were Greek, but around this time new settlers began to arrive. These were the Phoenicians, a nation of sea-traders who came from the coast of what is now Lebanon. Within 100 years, trade had grown remarkably and Cyprus became wealthy once again. However, the island also had several enemies. One by one, the people of Assyria (in western Asia), Egypt and Persia (present-day Iran) attacked Cyprus. The Persians finally conquered Cyprus in the sixth century BC.

In the Roman era, many Jews lived on Cyprus. The apostle Paul travelled to the island with his friend Barnabas to preach the word of Christ to the Jews. They arrived at Salamis, on the eastern coast, and gave sermons in the synagogue without success. Undeterred, they travelled throughout the island and finally arrived in Paphos on the west coast, where the Roman governor Sergius Paulus was interested in their message and asked them to preach. One of the people who worked for the governor was a Jewish magician called Elymas. Afraid of losing his job if the governor was influenced by the apostle, Elymas tried to distract the listeners. Paul was angered at this, and said that Elymas 'would be blinded'. Legend tells that at that moment, Elymas was blinded. The governor was amazed and became a Christian. Barnabas later became the first bishop of Cyprus.

The Romans

Alexander the Great ended Persian rule over Cyprus in 333 BC. The island first became part of the Macedonian Empire, and later of the Ptolemaean Empire, under the rule of the Egyptian king Ptolemy. At this time the Roman Empire was expanding and becoming the greatest that the world had ever known. Cyprus fell under Roman rule in the first century BC. Julius Caesar gave the island to Cleopatra of Egypt, but it effectively remained a province of Rome.

In Roman times, Cyprus was converted to Christianity by the apostle Paul and Saint Barnabas (see box). However, the early Christians were not very influential in Cyprus. The earliest monasteries and churches on the island only date back to the fourth century AD – hundreds of years after the island officially became Christian.

During the period of Roman rule, Cyprus suffered a series of natural disasters, including earthquakes, drought and famine, at the beginning of the fourth century AD. These destroyed many of the buildings, and even whole towns, and wreaked havoc among the population. Despite this, archeologists have uncovered many Roman buildings, including churches and theatres.

When the Roman Empire was divided in AD 395, Cyprus fell under Byzantine rule, which was governed from its capital, Constantinople.

▲ *The Romans built several open-air theatres (amphitheatres) on Cyprus. This one, at Kourion, had 17 rows of seats, which could accommodate 3,500 spectators.*

▶ *One of the first Christian churches on Cyprus can be found near Episkopi. This church was built in the fifth century AD. The palace of the bishop, of which very little remains today, was built close to this church. The word 'bishop' originates from 'Episkopi' ('episkopus' means 'overseer').*

▶ *The Stavrovouni monastery is located on a mountain-top at an altitude of 700 metres, on the outskirts of the Troödos mountain range. The mother of the Roman emperor Constantine the Great founded the monastery in AD 327. Women are forbidden from entering the monastery and are not allowed to approach closer than the car park.*

The Turks

In the seventh century, Cyprus was overrun by the Arabs from south-west Asia. They pillaged the entire island and established a garrison of 12,000 soldiers on the coast. These soldiers protected the Muslim Turks who now settled on the island. The Byzantine emperor and the leader of the Turks reached an agreement whereby they would jointly rule the island. This was an unusual arrangement, but it worked for 300 years. One effect of this, however, was that the Greek Cypriots moved inland and settled near Episkopi, while the Turks inhabited the coastal areas. The island's capital was moved to Nicosia, further inland.

Cyprus is situated close to the coast of Palestine, the 'Holy Land'. At the end of the eleventh century, this was under the control of the Muslim Turks and Christian countries began to launch 'Crusades' to drive out the Muslims and bring Christianity to Palestine. Cyprus was a strategic place for the Crusaders to set out on their journey to overthrow the Turks.

The holy capital Jerusalem was captured by the Crusaders in 1099. This, of course, angered the Turks and they began to attack. In the war that followed, Cyprus was removed from the Byzantine Empire. The Turkish leader, Isaac Commenus, declared himself emperor of Cyprus.

When the Arab leader Saladin recaptured Jerusalem in 1187, new Crusades were waged. Even kings and emperors – Louis VII of France and Emperor Conrad III of Germany – joined these crusades to help free Palestine.

◀ *Evidence of the Muslim Turks' rule on Cyprus can still be seen in mosques such as this one at Limassol.*

One of the countries involved in this next wave of Crusades was England, under its warrior king, Richard I (known as 'the Lionheart' because he was so fearless in battle). The king stopped on Cyprus on his way to the Holy Land in 1191. There he overthrew Commenus, and when he continued his journey the following year, he left behind troops to occupy the island.

The new English rulers immediately set about establishing their authority by raising taxes, which upset the local population. There followed a series of uprisings and King Richard began to think that his new territory was more trouble than it was worth. In 1192 he sold it to the Knights Templar, a special order of knights formed to protect Christian pilgrims travelling to the Holy Land.

Travelling with a fleet of ships from England to Palestine, King Richard the Lionheart found himself in a storm. The ships in his fleet became separated, and he landed in Limassol on Cyprus. He defeated the Cypriot ruler Isaac Commenus, who surrendered on condition that he was not bound in iron chains. Richard honoured the terms of the surrender – he bound Commenus in silver chains instead.

Also among the king's fleet was a ship carrying Richard's betrothed, Berengeria of Andria. The king decided to marry Berengeria in the castle at Limassol, and through this ceremony conducted on Cyprus, she became queen of England.

However, the Knights Templar also struggled with local uprisings, and it wasn't long before they passed control of Cyprus to a knight named Guy de Lusignan – a member of a French Catholic dynasty. This was the beginning of the Frankish occupation of the island, establishing the kingdom of Cyprus, with Guy de Lusignan as its king. Catholicism became the state religion.

▼ *The castle where Richard I, King of England, and Berengeria of Andria were married.*

▶ A sixteenth-century map of Cyprus. The coast of Turkey can be seen in the top left-hand corner. This map was made during the period of Turkish occupation on Cyprus.

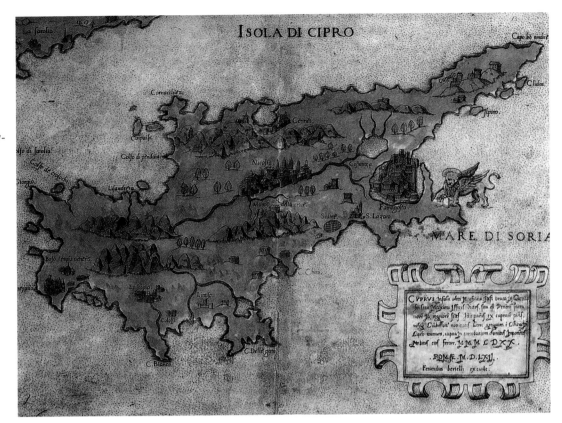

Attracted by the wealth of the island, new competitors, such as Genoa and Venice in Italy, made a bid for Cyprus. At the time, Italy did not exist as a single unified country but as a collection of 'city-states', each under its own rule. In 1489, the Venetians succeeded in gaining power over Cyprus. However, the Turkish Empire continued to fight for Cyprus and, 82 years later, succeeded in reoccupying the island. This brought an influx of colonists from Turkey to Cyprus.

Crown colony

The power of the Turks started to wane in the nineteenth century. Russia attacked, and the Greeks started their war of independence. The Turkish Empire was disintegrating. The English also started to take an interest in Cyprus because of its location close to the Suez Canal. The Suez Canal had been constructed in 1869 to provide a shorter route to India, which was a British colony at that time. The canal ran through northern Egypt, joining the Mediterranean with the Red Sea. The Turks and the British joined forces in 1878, and Turkey handed over Cyprus to British rule. From the island they could protect the Suez Canal from enemies much more easily.

The Greek Cypriots were happy under the British. Greece had won the war of independence and the Greek Cypriots hoped to be able to unite with liberated Greece. However, the Turkish Cypriots weren't prepared to do this.

After the First World War (1914–18), in which Turkey sided with Germany, Cyprus was annexed by Britain and became a Crown colony. The British continued to refuse the Greek Cypriots unification with Greece.

▲ Many signposts are still written in both Greek and English, even though Cyprus is no longer under British control.

The struggle continued for several years. After the Second World War (1939–45), a number of British colonies were granted independence, and this gave the Greek Cypriots hope that they might finally win their freedom. However, it became apparent that, as far as Britain and Turkey were concerned, unification with Greece was out of the question. The most attainable goal was the independence of Cyprus.

In 1955, civil war broke out, with left-wing parties fighting for the island's independence on one side, and the Orthodox Church – led by Archbishop Makarios – on the other side, fighting for unification with Greece.

▲ *This is part of the border dividing northern and southern Cyprus, cutting through the city of Nicosia. The northern part is largely Turkish Cypriot and the southern Greek Cypriot.*

Cyprus gained independence in 1960. In the new parliament, 70 per cent of the members were Greek Cypriots and 30 per cent were Turkish Cypriots. The president of the republic was Archbishop Makarios, and the Turkish Cypriot Fazil Kuchuk became vice-president. However, the 'troubles' between the Greek and Turkish Cypriots remained.

By 1974 Makarios was pursuing more neutral policies and wanted to peaceably resolve the differences between the Greek and Turkish Cypriots, so when Greece tried to force unification between Cyprus and Greece Makarios objected and demanded that Greek troops be withdrawn from the island. The Turks used this opportunity to gain control over the northern sector. About 180,000 people fled south.

Key figures in the Cypriot dispute

Makarios was born in 1913, in the village of Panayia in the Troödos mountain range, to the north-east of Paphos. When he was 13 years old, he became a novice in the Kykko monastery, where the monks were in favour of unification with Greece. He stayed until he was 26 years old, finishing his schooling there. Afterwards, he studied law and theology in Athens, where he was ordained as a priest in 1946. In 1948, he returned to Cyprus and became bishop of Larnaca. He assumed the name of his predecessor Makarios II, and became Makarios III.

At first he wanted to see Cyprus unified with Greece, and travelled around widely to gain support for his campaign. In 1960, he was elected as the first president of Cyprus. He was re-elected by a large majority in 1968 and again in 1973. Slowly, he began to promote the idea of an independent Cyprus. After the Turkish coup in 1974, Makarios fled to England by way of Malta, but he returned to Cyprus a few months later. He died in 1977. The present leader of the Greek Cypriots in southern Cyprus is Tassos Papadopoulos.

▲ *Archbishop Makarios, who became the first president of Cyprus after it gained independence in 1960.*

Rauf Denktas is the president of the Turkish Republic of Northern Cyprus. He was born in 1924, in the village of Baf, not far from Paphos. He grew up in a wealthy Islamic family. He attended the British grammar school on Cyprus and went on to study law in London.

Denktas became politically active and acted as a negotiator on behalf of the Turkish Cypriots with the Greek Cypriots in 1968. He was made president in the wake of the occupation of northern Cyprus in 1974 and still holds the position today. Denktas adheres strongly to his principles and will not accept that a unified Cyprus is an option.

A united Cyprus?

Efforts are still being made to unite the two halves of Cyprus. Kofi Annan, Secretary General of the United Nations, has succeeded in getting the two parties back to the negotiating table. In a referendum in March 2004, 60 per cent of the Turkish Cypriot population voted in favour of a united Cyprus. Unfortunately, the Greek Cypriot population voted against unification, so the country remains divided. On 1 May 2004, only the Greek Cypriot part of the island became a member of the European Union.

▲ *Rauf Denktas, the current president of northern Cyprus.*

▼ *A street café in the capital. Its name, 'Berlin', reflects the divided status of Nicosia. The city of Berlin in Germany was split in two after the Second World War.*

The country

Cyprus lies in the Mediterranean Sea, and despite its long association with Greece, it is actually closer to Asia than to Europe. The island is 230 km long (east to west) and about 80 km wide (north to south). It is the third-largest island in the Mediterranean Sea, after Sicily and Sardinia.

▼ *The Troödos mountain range. In the foreground are the fertile valleys that provide good farming land.*

Cyprus has a surface area of 9,300 km². Over three-quarters of the population is Greek – around 600,000 people live in the southern part of the island. The northern sector is inhabited largely by the Turkish Cypriots, who number around 140,000. The population density is about 83 people per square kilometre.

The landscape on Cyprus is diverse. The 648 km of coastline have both sand and shingle beaches, open bays and steep cliffs. The interior is characterised by high mountain ranges, hilly countryside and broad plains.

Mountains

There are two mountain ranges in Cyprus – Troödos and Kirenia – which cross the island from east to west. The highest peak, Olympus (1,953 metres), lies in the Troödos range in the south-west of the country. This mountain range rises very gradually. In the northern part of Cyprus lies the the lower Kirenia mountain range, which is largely made up of limestone. Pine trees grow on the mountains. Between these two ranges lies the Mesaoria, a broad flat plain that serves as the country's main agricultural region.

▼ *The reservoir of the Kouris Dam, near Alassa.*

As the snow melts in the mountains, it cascades downwards, creating streams, rivers and sometimes even waterfalls.

ΚΑΤΑΡΡΑΚΤΗΣ ΚΑΛΗΔΟΝΙΩΝ

KALEDONIA FALLS 1 KM

E4

Rivers and forests

Most of the rivers on Cyprus are quite small. The largest is the Kouris River, in the west of the island. In springtime, when the snow melts on the mountain-tops, a lot of water flows down through these small rivers. To control the flow of water, dams have been built across several rivers in Cyprus.

In ancient times there used to be many forests on Cyprus, but over the years forest fires and extensive deforestation have left the mountain slopes quite bare. In more recent times efforts have been made to rectify this situation. Schemes were introduced to plant new trees – many of which have now grown to full size. Today, one fifth of the island is covered in forest once again. This is especially important in the mountains, where natural forests have now grown back, providing a habitat for many rare plants and animals.

Coastline

The southern coast of Cyprus has a number of broad bays and the main harbours – Paphos, Larnaca and Limassol – are located there. There are also many sandy beaches along the coastline, and these, together with the warm Mediterranean climate, attract thousands of holiday-makers every year. Some of the coastline is more dramatic, though, with rugged cliffs and huge rocks in the water where the coastline has been eroded over many centuries.

Climate

Cyprus is the hottest and driest island in the Mediterranean Sea. It has long, dry summers and mild winters. The hottest months are July and August, when temperatures can reach 40°C. The average temperature in summer, however, is about 30°C. Because it can get so hot, it is best to visit Cyprus between March and the end of May, or in September and October. In these months it is pleasantly warm, with temperatures of about 25°C. The winter months – December, January and February – are usually rainy and windy, with average temperatures of 12°C.

High up in the mountains it can get extremely cold. In winter, there is often snow on the higher slopes. In January, it is sometimes possible to go swimming in the sea on the south coast, and go skiing in the mountains a few hours later! In the winter months there is an average of 400 mm of rainfall, with up to 1,100 mm in the west. For the rest of the year it almost always remains dry.

▼ *Turtle Beach in northern Cyprus is protected during the summer months, when the turtles come here to lay their eggs.*

▼ *Between December and January, rainfall can be so heavy that it causes flooding in the streets.*

Towns and cities

Cyprus's capital city, Nicosia, is the dividing point between the northern (Turkish) and southern (Greek) populations. As such, armed soldiers can be seen patrolling the streets on both sides of this ancient city. It is the largest city on the island, with around 230,000 inhabitants. Its Greek name is Lefkosia.

Nicosia

Nicosia has been the capital of Cyprus since the seventh century. When the country was partitioned in 1974 after the civil war, a British army officer – charged with keeping the militant Turks and Greeks apart – used a green pen to mark a line on a map to indicate the boundary. This line ran straight through Nicosia, and the boundary is still known as the 'Green Line'. The line is now marked by a wall of barrels (see page 12) and is guarded by United Nations checkpoints.

It is difficult to get to southern Cyprus from the northern part, as the border between these two sectors of the island is closed. There is one point in Nicosia where the border can be crossed, but only under certain conditions and for a controlled length of time.

Under the rule of the Lusignans in the fifteenth and sixteenth centuries, many palaces, mansions, churches and monasteries were built in the town. However, when the Venetians took over, they tore down many of these old buildings, although some remains can still be seen today.

The oldest part of the city, Laïki Geitonia, had grown rather dilapidated, but a renovation programme was initiated and it is now a shopping centre with a pedestrian area.

◄ *The pedestrian area in Laïki Geitonia is part of the recent renovation of the older parts of the city.*

Nico and his friend are waiting for their girlfriends, who have gone shopping in Nicosia. 'The girls want to buy new clothes,' he says. 'There are plenty of clothes shops here. You can buy all the big brands, even the quite expensive ones.'

There isn't often trouble in this divided city, although sometimes fanatics try to provoke people. 'Usually there are tourists who want to see the border and wander about the old town. We prefer to go out in the new town. When the girls get back we'll go for a drink in an outdoor café.'

Larnaca

Larnaca (or Larnaka) lies on the southern coast of Cyprus. It is the third-largest city on the island, with around 74,000 inhabitants, and it is a flourishing city. The main airport in Cyprus once lay near Nicosia, but this has now been closed down and the new airport is situated near Larnaca. This means that the city enjoys much tourist trade. Many refugees from other countries have also settled here.

▼ The salt-lake near Larnaca lies three metres below sea level.

The northern part of Larnaca has been built on the ruins of the old city, Kition. This has been a thriving port town since Roman times and throughout the centuries the harbour has been used to trade in two of Cyprus's most important exports – copper and salt.

Although salt is no longer an important source of income for the island, it used to be very valuable. The salt came from the large salt-lake that lies close to Larnaca. In the summer, the water in the lake evaporates and leaves an enormous basin of salt.

◀ *The interior of the Djami Kebir mosque, on the coast near Larnaca. The mosque was built in the sixteenth century and is still in use today.*

There are several fine old buildings in this area, including a Turkish fort dating from 1605 and a mosque from the sixteenth century, both situated on the coast. The church of St Lazarus can be found further inland.

One of the legends associated with Larnaca relates to a story from the Bible. A man named Lazarus had died and been buried. Four days after his burial, Jesus visited his tomb and raised him from the dead. The story goes that Lazarus boarded a ship to Cyprus and first set foot on the island near Larnaca. He established a church there and became the bishop of Kition.

▼ *The church of St Lazarus was built above the saint's 'second grave'. According to the Bible, Lazarus was brought back to life by Jesus.*

Limassol

Limassol (or Lemessos) is the second-largest city on Cyprus, with about 165,000 inhabitants. It has the biggest harbour on the island and is also the most important tourist resort. The old city centre is small and rather cluttered, but it has more modern sections as well. The most attractive things about the city are the nearby beaches and the views across the harbour. When the harbour at Famagusta was closed, much of its trade was adopted by Limassol and it is now a thriving port.

Limassol is also a centre of light industry, including wineries and fruit-juice factories. Many shops in town sell articles made of leather, such as bags, backpacks, shoes and coats. However, because of the tourists, local shopkeepers tend to sell more souvenirs than local handicrafts. Along the palm-bordered promenade, which runs for several kilometres, there are hotels, restaurants and small supermarkets. Throughout the year, tourists can be found enjoying the views along this stretch.

▶ *The promenade along the shoreline. Further off, ships are at anchor, waiting to dock in the harbour.*

▼ *A view across Limassol, looking towards the mountains.*

Paphos

Paphos, on the west coast of Cyprus, has around 49,000 inhabitants, and is the smallest of the four large cities on the island. Paphos has two parts – the lower town, Kato Paphos, and the upper town, Ktima. There has been a settlement here since ancient times, when it was known as Paleo Paphos ('Old Paphos'). By 1300 BC the city had become known as a centre for the worship of the goddess Aphrodite (see page 45). It remained a focus for pilgrimage until the fourth century AD, when Christianity was finally adopted on the island. Paphos later developed into a small harbour town for Crusaders, but after that it declined dramatically and by the nineteenth century it only had around 2,000 inhabitants.

Today Paphos is an important tourist resort. The most interesting historical remains are found in the lower town. These include an early Christian basilica, the ruins of several Roman villas with well-preserved mosaics, and a number of tombs. The Sanctuary of Aphrodite is situated roughly 12 km from Paphos, near the village of Konklia.

Kyrenia

Kyrenia lies on the north coast. Its situation – between the Mediterranean Sea and the group of mountains known as Besparmark ('five fingers') to the south – has made this one of the most popular spots on the island. There is a splendid view of the old city from the mountains. In the old harbour there are both fishing boats and pleasure yachts. One of the most fascinating sights is the old castle, situated in the harbour, which was built in the Byzantine period on the ruins of a Roman fortress. The Lusignan rulers expanded and fortified it over the years, and this work was continued by the Venetians when they gained control of Cyprus. On a nearby mountain stands the castle of St Hilarion. This was built by the Byzantines and was used by the Lusignan rulers as their summer residence.

◀ *This huge amphora (jug) was discovered during an excavation in Paphos. Such jugs were used by the ancient Greeks and Romans for carrying wine.*

Léfkara

Léfkara is one of the most famous villages in Cyprus. It is situated on the lower slopes of the Troödos mountain range, at an altitude of about 730 metres. The village has two centres – Páno Léfkara (upper) and Káto Léfkara (lower). The name of the village originated from the word *lefkaritiko*, which means 'open piece of embroidery', and it is because of the beautiful embroidery created by the locals that the village is so well-known.

The houses in the village are often set up as little shops, since the women not only embroider for pleasure, but also sell their handiwork. Many years ago, the men of the village would work as salesmen, travelling through Europe carrying samples of embroidery that their wives, mothers and sisters had made at Léfkara. They wrote down the orders and back home the women produced the goods.

Nowadays, the men do not have to travel to sell the wares. The demand is so great that the women cannot keep up with it. It has become an industry in itself. Every city on Cyprus has a shop selling handiwork from Léfkara. Silver products made in Léfkara are also sold in other cities on Cyprus.

◄ *Léfkara is not only famous for its embroidery – the village also has a silversmith who sits outside and fashions pieces of jewellery and other items out of silver, which the women then sell in their shops.*

▼ *The village Káto Léfkara, situated on a gentle slope in the Troödos mountains.*

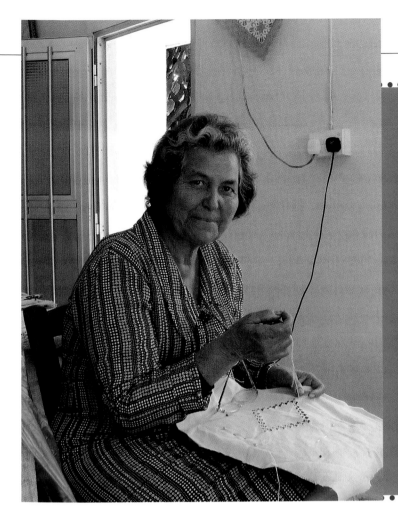

This is Andrea. She owns a traditional embroidery shop in Léfkara. 'I learned embroidery from my mother,' she explains. 'When I was young, we would do embroidery at home. My mother was taught by her mother, and she was taught by her mother, and so on. This has been our tradition for centuries. I am now teaching my daughter to embroider.' Her daughter walks into the shop at that moment. She sits down in the sun, and takes out her embroidery. Andrea takes a one-pound note from her purse, and smoothes it out. She points out the image on the banknote. 'Look. That is a drawing of our village, Léfkara. There is also a piece of embroidery on the note.' She walks over to the counter, and shows us an identical piece of embroidery.

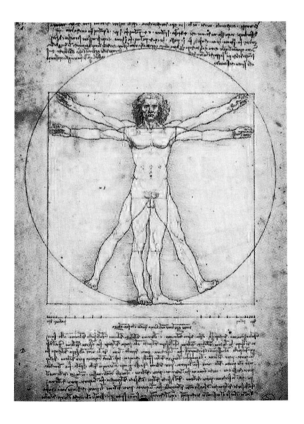

It is said that Leonardo da Vinci (1451–1519) visited Léfkara in 1481. He had been assigned the task of buying a new altar-cloth for Milan Cathedral. Venetian tradesmen had told him that he could find beautifully embroidered cloths in Léfkara. He decided to travel to Cyprus, and commissioned the women of the village to make a large altar-cloth for the cathedral.

Leonardo da Vinci is best remembered for his paintings, in particular the *Mona Lisa*, but he was also responsible for designing some inventions that would have been unimaginable in his time. Among his drawings were designs for a kind of helicopter, a parachute and a diving-suit. The picture (left) shows the Vitruvian Man, and is a study of the perfect proportions of the human body.

People and culture

The population of Cyprus is approximately 780,000. Of this, 77 per cent are Greek Cypriot and 18 per cent Turkish Cypriot. The remaining 5 per cent is made up of foreign residents. The official languages are Greek and Turkish, but English is also spoken by many people on the island.

▼ *The population of Cyprus has grown dramatically since the nineteenth century.*

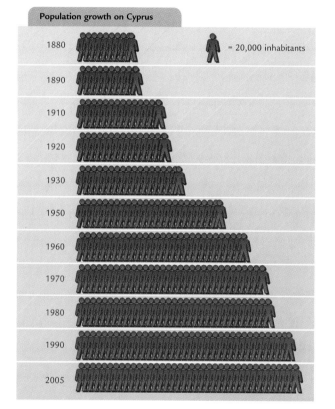

Population growth on Cyprus

1880	
1890	
1910	
1920	
1930	
1950	
1960	
1970	
1980	
1990	
2005	

= 20,000 inhabitants

Tourism is an important industry for Cyprus. Many of the towns and cities are geared towards tourists, and they are usually made welcome across Cyprus. Many Cypriots like to practise their English and enjoy chatting to visitors.

Because the weather is usually good, people on Cyprus spend most of their time outdoors. At the weekends many families take trips to the beaches or to sites of historical interest. The Cypriot people enjoy close family ties.

Religion

The Greek population of Cyprus, in the southern sector, is almost entirely Greek Orthodox. This Church is one of the Eastern Orthodox denominations, and is autonomous – it works under a system of self-government.

Members of the Greek Orthodox Church are led by patriarchs and archbishops. Archbishop Makarios (see page 12) was both the spiritual leader of the Church and the political leader of the country.

Monasteries are important in the Eastern Orthodox Church, and they have long been a significant part of religious life on Cyprus. Although many of the ancient monasteries are now little more than ruins, there are still around 10 active monasteries on the island.

◄ *A shopkeeper and his friend pass the time of day on the street outside the shop.*

Petros is walking along the promenade near Limassol. He isn't looking around, but keeps his eyes on the ground. He explains what he is doing. 'No,' he says, laughing. 'I haven't lost anything – but I am looking for something.'

He opens his hand, revealing dark-coloured seeds. He points at a tree with his other hand. 'My wife puts these seeds into cakes,' he tells us. 'It tastes very good! You have to peel them first, to reveal a white nut which you can put into the batter. Well, not me, of course, but my wife. I can't bake to save my life, but I can look for these seeds.'

The tree is a pine tree. The seeds are pine seeds or pine nuts and they are a popular ingredient in Cypriot cooking.

▲ *Petros searches the ground for pine seeds to take home to his wife. She uses them in her baking.*

▼ *This mosque stands in the Turkish sector of the Cypriot capital Nicosia, where most people are Muslims.*

The Turkish Cypriots, in the northern part of the island, are Muslims, and live according to the laws of Islam. The northern sector is scattered with mosques, where the Muslims worship.

Among the minority groups on Cyprus (which make up around 5 per cent of the population) are the Armenians. These people are members of the Armenian Church, which has about 2,000 members.

There is also a Maronite Church – another Christian sect – with about 7,000 members. Most of these are of Lebanese descent. This Church was established in Cyprus in the ninth century AD.

◄ *The modern building that houses the Cyprus Broadcasting Corporation in Nicosia.*

Media

The national broadcasting company in southern Cyprus is the Cyprus Broadcasting Corporation, which airs programmes on two channels, RIK 1 and RIK 2. There are also a number of commercial channels, such as Lumiere TV and Sigma International TV. A few cities have local or regional broadcasting companies. The Cyprus Broadcasting Corporation also runs several radio stations. Radio 1 and Radio 3 broadcast in Greek, and Radio 2 broadcasts in Greek, English and Armenian. There are also commercial and regional radio stations. In the north there is Bayrak Radyo Televizyon Kurumu, which airs both Turkish and English programmes. Akdeniz TV is a Turkish television station, and there are also some Turkish radio stations. Cyprus has both Greek and English newspapers – the *Simerini* and the *Cyprus Mail* and *Cyprus News* respectively. In the north there are the Turkish newspapers, *Halkin Sesi* and *Kibris Gazetesi*.

Government

On 15 November 1983, Rauf Denktas declared the Turkish zone of Cyprus a sovereign and independent state. The new state was recognised by Turkey. However, the Greek Cypriots still consider Cyprus as part of a unified republic. Every five years, the Greek Cypriot population elects a president, who is both head of state and the chairman of the council, which consists of 11 ministers. There are three large political parties and a number of smaller ones. The most important parties are the Democratic Rally (DISY), which is a conservative right-wing party, the Progressive Labour Party (AKEL) and the Democratic Party (DIKO), all of which are Greek Cypriot. According to the Cypriot Constitution, the parliament must comprise 80 members. Every five years, the Greek Cypriots elect 56 of these members of parliament, and the Turkish Cypriots elect 24. However, the Turkish Cypriot members have not been elected since 1964. The Turkish Cypriots boycotted parliament, and the northern part of Cyprus has had its own parliament since 1985.

▼ *The presidential palace in Nicosia, home of the reigning Greek Cypriot head of state.*

Education

The education system in southern Cyprus dates from the time of British rule, and has many similarities with the system in the UK. In the Turkish part of the island, the school system is closer to that in Turkey.

For Greek Cypriots, school attendance is compulsory between the ages of six and 15. Six-year-olds first go to primary school for six years, before moving on to secondary education, which also lasts six years. In the first three years of secondary school, all children follow a grammar-school curriculum, in which they study a wide range of subjects. After that, they can choose to go to a technical secondary school to receive vocational training, or to an upper secondary school. Diplomas from either of these can gain students entry to university.

◀ These girls attend a grammar school in Limassol (above). They wear a school uniform consisting of a grey pleated skirt and a blue top. Uniforms are a British tradition, which has remained from the time when Cyprus was a British colony.

▼ *A Cypriot text book about the history of the island.*

▲ *The University of Cyprus is based in the capital Nicosia, but it does not yet offer the range of subjects available at universities in the UK.*

The University of Cyprus established a number of faculties in Nicosia in 1992. Here, students can study economics, engineering, literature, biology, physics and chemistry. For most other studies students have to go abroad (often to Athens, London or the United States). There is also a general polytechnic, a polytechnic for forestry, tourism and trade, as well as training for teachers and the medical professions.

▼ *These primary-school children are on a field trip to an excavation site near Choirokoitia.*

The system in northern Cyprus is different from that in the south. Here, children attend kindergarten from the age of five. They move on to primary school when they are seven, and primary education lasts for five years, until pupils are 12 years old. Primary education is free and compulsory for all children.

After this, children attend the first phase of secondary education – junior-secondary – which lasts three years. Pupils are 15 years old when they complete this phase. Between the ages of 16 and 18, students can choose to do a three-year educational programme in either high schools (called lycees), which are similar to grammar schools, or at vocational schools. At the vocational secondary schools, students learn specific skills such as agriculture, nursing or hotel management.

In northern Cyprus there is the University of Turkish Cyprus, located in Famagusta. However, because this is the only university in the region, many students choose to continue their education in other countries – often Turkey.

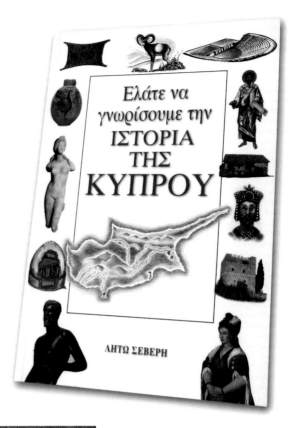

▲ Books like this are used in primary schools.

◄ These boys are enjoying their school trip. Although the education systems in northern and southern Cyprus are different, children from both regions learn about the ancient history of the island as well as about the modern politics that have divided it.

Cuisine

Traditional cuisine on Cyprus has largely been influenced by Greece and Turkey. One of the most popular specialities that has come from these countries is meze.

Meze is a selection of different dishes. When you order meze in a restaurant you get about 20 small courses of all different varieties, including meat, fish, vegetables and fruit.

▼ *Many British people visit the island. Lots of restaurants serve an 'English breakfast' — scrambled eggs, poached or fried eggs with bacon, toast, sausages and baked beans.*

▲ *Commandaria wine is a famous Cypriot export.*

▲ *Restaurants describe their meze on these signs. This restaurant also serves kleftiko, which is a leg of lamb, roasted in the oven with garlic, rosemary, oregano and mint.*

Recipe for tzatziki

Ingredients
1 cucumber
Greek or Turkish yoghurt
Mint
Oregano
Olive oil
Garlic
Salt

Finely grate the cucumber into a sieve and sprinkle lightly with salt. Let it drain and then pat dry. Put the yoghurt in a bowl and add two chopped cloves of garlic. Add the drained cucumber and season with finely chopped mint, salt and pepper. You can also add dried oregano. Blend in the olive oil and stir well. Enjoy it as a tasty bread-dip!

Meze

Normally, a plate of hot bread is served first, and a large bowl with a salad of tomatoes, onion and feta cheese, together with a few dips, such as táhini, which is made from sesame seeds. Next, a series of cold dishes is served. These often include tzatziki, tarama (made of fish-roe) and koupépia (stuffed vine leaves). After the cold dishes come small plates containing hot dishes, such as souvlaki (pork or lamb served in pitta bread), afélia (meat stewed in wine) and klefthédes (fried meatballs). Although the servings are quite small, meze can be very filling. Some restaurants serve a 'meze' of fish dishes and a 'meze' of vegetarian dishes.

Fish

Fish stocks around Cyprus have increased in recent years, because over-fishing has become less widespread. Cyprus also imports a lot of frozen fish. However, fresh fish remains a popular dish on the island and there are a few trout farms in the Troödos mountains.

Wine

Plenty of wine is produced on Cyprus – both white and red. The Commandaria, a sweet dessert wine, is very famous, and it has been made on the island since ancient times, when it was drunk during the festivals to honour Aphrodite (see page 46). The Crusaders also loved it, and established large vineyards on the island. The grapes are gathered as late as possible, and are dried in the sun before they are pressed.

▼ *A trout farm near the Kaledonia Waterfalls.*

Transport

Travelling around Cyprus is easy, as the roads are well-maintained and public transport is good between and within the major cities.

▼ Bus services are good between larger cities, but travelling to the smaller villages by public transport can be difficult.

Buses and roads

Bus transport to and from the tourist resorts and the big cities and towns is good on Cyprus. However, the buses are not so reliable elsewhere on the island. The villages in the interior of the island can only be reached by bus once or twice a day, and some cannot be reached by public transport at all. The best way to visit these places is to hire a car.

The roads on Cyprus are good. Motorways run between the larger cities and the smaller roads are well-maintained. The speed limit on the motorways is 100 kph, and there are many speed checks. On two-lane roads, the speed limit is 80 kph, and in towns it is 50 kph. Cyprus used to be a British colony, and Cypriots still drive on the left-hand side of the road.

▶ The roads on Cyprus are well marked, and destinations are also given in English.

▼ This motorway runs between the key cities of Paphos and Larnaca.

▶ *Limassol is a busy harbour and often ships have to wait some distance offshore until it is their turn to dock.*

Ferries

Taking a boat is the best way to travel between Cyprus and the mainland. There are ferries to Cyprus from Athens and Rhodes in Greece. There is also a boat connection to Haifa in Israel. There is another ferry connection from Mersin in southern Turkey to the Turkish part of Cyprus.

Aviation

Cyprus has two airline companies. The main one is Cyprus Airways, which works in co-operation with other airlines such as the Dutch airline KLM. The other airline, in northern Cyprus, is Cyprus-Turkish Airlines. There are three international airports on Cyprus, one near Larnaca, one near Paphos and a third near Ercan in the north. Since the old airport in Nicosia was closed in 1974, the one near Larnaca has become the largest and most frequently used. Larnaca lies about 50 km from the capital.

The area around Paphos has become an important tourist resort. As a consequence, the airport has undergone expansion over the last few years. It is situated about 10 km from the city.

▼ *The main airline company, Cyprus Airways flies to and from several European destinations from Larnaca International Airport.*

The economy

Since Cyprus gained independence in 1960, the economy has grown quite quickly, and emigration and unemployment have decreased. The Greek Cypriots have profited most from this development.

▼ *Wine is an important export for Cyprus. This woman is taking a break from harvesting the grapes that will be made into wine.*

Since the formal division of Cyprus into a Greek part and a Turkish part in 1974, the gap between the two economies has widened. Immediately after the division there was a large economic recession. The Greek part of Cyprus recovered more quickly, growing at about 4 per cent each year.

The number of workers participating in agriculture (32 per cent in the Turkish part and 13 per cent in the Greek part) has dropped because of the growing economy, building industry, trade and tourism.

▼ *This is one of the largest asbestos mines in Europe, in the Troödos mountains on Cyprus. The mine was closed in 1988 because there was little demand for asbestos, and exposure to it can cause cancer. The closure of the mine resulted in a drop in the mining industry's contribution to Cyprus's economy.*

Trade

Cyprus has many trading partners within the European Union, which the country joined in 2004. More than half of Cyprus's trade is with the UK, Italy, Greece and Germany.

Textile products are the most important export from Cyprus, followed by potatoes, shoes, concrete and raw materials. These raw materials include copper, iron, chrome ores, marble and gypsum (plaster of Paris), and all are extracted from mines on Cyprus. The island also exports canned fruit, wine, vegetables and olive oil. Many of these goods are destined for Greece, the UK and some of the Arab countries.

The main imported products are foodstuffs, petroleum and petroleum products, machines and chemical products. The main suppliers are the UK, the USA, Germany, Greece and Italy.

Industry

Most of the industrial activity on Cyprus can be found near the larger towns. Here, Cyprus's main agricultural products are processed: olives are pressed into oil, vegetables and fruits are canned, wine and juice are bottled. On a smaller scale, clothing, textiles and leather are produced. All this happens in factories, usually situated on the outskirts of the cities.

The economy of the Turkish part of the island is focused almost exclusively on Turkey. It is cut off from a lot of international aid and from exporting opportunities (since 1983, the European Union has only imported goods from the Greek part). Consequently, the economic growth of the Turkish sector has been significantly less than the growth of the Greek Cypriot economy. Northern Cyprus remains largely agricultural.

▲ *Industrial cranes in the port of Larnaca. These are used to load and unload ships that travel to and from Cyprus's trading partners.*

Agriculture and cattle-breeding

Nearly 50 per cent of Cyprus is arable land, and corn is the most common crop. Potatoes and subtropical fruits are also common. Cyprus exports a lot of fruit and vegetables, including almonds, figs and carrots. Cotton is also grown and exported. The farms are often small family businesses.

The most important agricultural area in Cyprus is the fertile plain of Mesaoria, to the east of Nicosia. The people of Cyprus used to raise goats and sheep for their own use. Today they breed cows and sheep to sell milk, meat and other dairy products. There are also pig and poultry farms, which are developing modern production methods and marketing. Due to effective EU regulations, fishing is improving as well. About 2,700 tonnes of fish are processed each year. Because of improved techniques (refrigeration, etc.), the fish can even be exported.

▲ *The harbours are usually bustling with activity, as the fishermen check the day's catch.*

▼ *These terraces on the hillsides are growing grapes, which will be made into wine.*

Tourism

Tourism is one of the most important parts of Cyprus's economy, and more than 12 per cent of the gross domestic product of Cyprus is generated by tourists.

In 2002, 2,418,233 tourists visited the southern part of Cyprus. In the year 2000 there were 2,686,205 tourists.

Many Turks spend their holidays in the northern part of Cyprus. In 1999 414,000 tourists visited northern Cyprus, of which 335,000 were Turkish; 79,000 people visited from other countries.

▲ The beach at Protaras, not far from Larnaca, in the south-eastern leg of the island.

▼ There are many ancient buildings for visitors to see on Cyprus. These mosaics date from Roman times.

▲ The promenade at Limassol is a popular place for tourists to take a stroll and admire the view across the harbour.

▼ *Cyprus's magnificent beaches draw thousands of visitors every year.*

The average tourist stays on Cyprus for just over ten days. Before 1974, the most important tourist resorts were Famagusta and Kyrenia in northern Cyprus. However, since the division of the island, a large part of the tourist trade has moved to the southern coastal area.

Paphos, Limassol and Larnaca are now the most important tourist resorts. Many hotels have been built on the promenade in Limassol. There are also large apartment blocks, where it is possible to rent an apartment for a night, a week, or even the whole year. Many Scandinavians and British people spend the winter here in the Mediterranean climate.

▼ *An apartment block near Limassol. Hotels and apartment blocks can be found everywhere in Cyprus.*

▲ *Even in winter, the beach is a pleasant place to be.*

Andreos is enjoying the sun. He has finished working for the day, and is watching people pass by. 'In the summer, the streets are full of tourists,' he says. He does not mind at all – he is used to it. 'They're not noisy or rude, either. Well, there is the occasional exception, youngsters mostly, but here, in the street where I live, it's generally quiet.' In the evening, most tourists go to the promenade, where the majority of restaurants and pubs can be found.

Many restaurants, terraces and shops selling souvenirs have been built to accommodate the tourists. Embroidery from Léfkara is very popular, and is a real example of Cypriot crafts (see page 22). Other traditional handicrafts include leather goods and silverware.

◀ ▲ The Hospitaller Knights (Knights of St John) built the Kolossi Castle in the twelfth century. Large parts of it are still standing.

Kolossi Castle

The Kolossi Castle is situated close to Limassol on the edge of the Akotiri Peninsula, and is one of the most popular spots for tourists. The castle was built by the Hospitaller Knights as a refuge for Crusaders who had been driven away from Palestine. The Knight Hospitaller Order, also known as the Knights of St John, was a religious order of warrior monks. When the first Crusades started around 1100, they took care of the wounded, but were equally devout soldiers.

The order lived in the Kolossi Castle until 1488. It was conquered by the Venetians in that year and by the Turks 90 years later. During their time in the castle, the knights leased the land around the castle to tenants, who grew cotton, grapes and sugar-cane there. The order even established a sugar factory. Commandaria wine (see page 30) was once produced in a winery there.

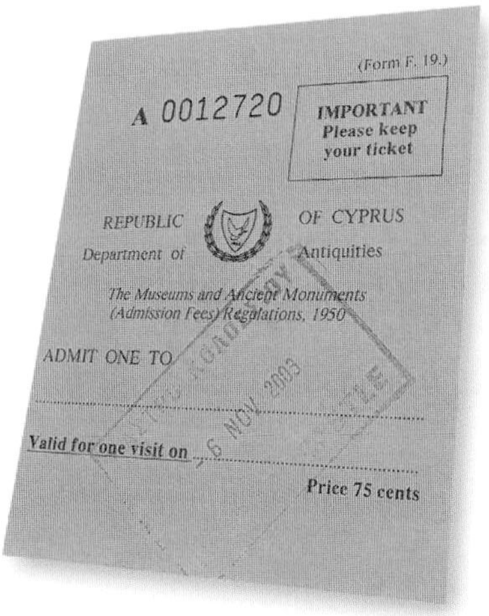

▲ An admission ticket to the Kolossi Castle; it costs 75 cents.

▶ The tomb of Umm-Haram, the aunt of the Prophet Mohammed, in the mosque near Larnaca.

Hala Sultan Tekkesi mosque

On the shores of the large salt-lake near Larnaca (see page 18) lies the Hala Sultan Tekkesi mosque. This is regarded as one of most important sanctuaries in the Islamic religion. It contains the tomb of Umm Haram, who was the aunt of the Prophet Mohammed.

Umm Haram and her husband are said to have visited Cyprus in AD 694. According to legend, she fell from her mule and died. She was buried in the place she fell.

A shrine was built many centuries later, in 1760, by Sheikh Hasan. This was shortly followed by the mosque itself, intended to permanently mark the spot and provide a focus for pilgrimage. A fountain was later built in the courtyard of the mosque. The mosque is currently undergoing restoration work to make sure it remains one of the most beautiful and important places for Muslims to come and pay homage.

From a plane flying into Larnaca Airport, it is possible to see the mosque on the shore of the salt-lake. There is a legend about how the salt-lake came into being, based in the Christian tradition. The biblical figure Lazarus wandered through this area, and was very thirsty. He passed a large vineyard. The female owner had just gathered grapes, and had put them in a covered basket. Lazarus asked her for a few grapes. She answered that the basket held not grapes but salt, and refused to give him anything. As punishment, her vineyard was flooded by the salty water of the ocean, creating the salt-lake that lies there today.

◀ The Hala Sultan Tekkesi mosque stands on the edge of the salt-lake near Larnaca.

Nature

▼ *There are many different trees on Cyprus, including orange and olive trees, as well as grapevines.*

There are several areas of natural beauty on Cyprus and the island abounds with diverse species of flora and fauna. The mountainous regions in particular are home to wild animals and a variety of trees and plants.

Trees

Although a great many trees were planted on Cyprus in the twentieth century, there are more that are older still. Several of the cedar trees, in particular, are centuries old. There is a cedar valley in the west of the island, which contains a forest with about 50,000 cedar trees. The oldest trees in the forest are believed to be more than 850 years old.

There are also many pine trees on Cyprus, particularly in the mountains. There are large vineyards on the western and southern slopes of the Troödos mountain range, where, among other things, the well-known Commandaria wine is made. Further down on these slopes you can find acacia, cypress, olive and carob trees.

There are poplars and eucalyptus trees in the valleys, as well as orchards where pears, apples, cherries, peaches, almonds and walnuts are grown. Palm trees and agaves are especially common near the coast. A lot of plants bloom from February to May, such as daffodils, cyclamen, irises, orchids, anemones, poppies, turban buttercups and peonies.

Animals

One of the most famous mammals is the moufflon, a type of sheep. It is now a protected species. There are other small mammals, such as foxes, rabbits, weasels and hares, as well as different species of bats, snakes, lizards, turtles, frogs and chameleons. Cyprus is home to more than 50 species of butterfly.

On the southern coast of Cyprus, a skeleton has been found, which experts believe to be that of a pygmy hippo. This animal has now been hunted to extinction.

▲ *The moufflon is Cyprus's national symbol and is found in the mountain regions. The males have long curling horns.*

There is a saying that goes 'the only good snake is a dead snake'. A lot of people are afraid of snakes. However, snakes are actually more afraid of humans, and will usually only bite when they feel threatened. The asp is the only poisonous snake on Cyprus. The lack of snakes on the island is probably due to St Helena, mother of the Roman emperor Constantine the Great, who lived in the fourth century AD. She brought cats to the monastery of St Nicholas to keep poisonous snakes away. The cats have done a good job, as poisonous snakes are now very rarely seen near the monastery.

Mediterranean monk seals and dolphins are protected species. In summer, scaly turtles – another protected species – deposit their eggs in the sand on the beaches.

Fish

There are no fish in the small streams in the mountains, only in the larger rivers. However, there are many freshwater crabs in the streams. In the reservoirs at the Germasogeia Dam and Kouris Dam, there are freshwater fish such as carp, perch and trout.

There was a period in which overfishing resulted in almost empty waters in the sea round the island. Since measures were taken to stop overfishing, however, fish stocks have slowly increased. Many of these measures were instigated by the European Union, and fishermen now have to comply with EU guidelines when out fishing. The most common fish are parrot fish, European blennies, gobies and rainbow fish.

Several national parks and nature reserves have been established in the last few years. The Athalasa and Tripylos National Parks in the Troödos mountain range are two of the most important, and many rare plants and animals are protected in these areas.

Birds

From the end of August onwards, migrating birds such as storks, buzzards, kites, falcons, common cranes, and many songbirds and water birds come to Cyprus. One of the most amazing sights is the flock of flamingos that spends its winters in the salt-lakes. In recent years, the number of flamingos in the flock has decreased from 18,000 to about 3,000. This is probably because the salt-lake has remained dry for the last few years instead of filling up in the winter as it used to do.

A bird of prey common on Cyprus is the Bonelli's eagle. This bird can also be seen in southern Europe and Africa. The griffon vulture can also be spotted on occasion.

▼ *The Cyprus warbler is native to the island. During the winter it migrates to the nearby mainland of Israel or Egypt.*

Mythology

Aphrodite is the goddess of love in ancient Greek mythology, and legends about her, and several other gods, have had a long association with Cyprus.

▲▼ *These urns were found near the Sanctuary of Aphrodite. The ancient Greeks kept wine in them.*

One of the deities worshipped on Cyprus was the goddess Astarte. She was originally the Phoenician goddess of fertility. When the Greeks arrived on Cyprus, they incorporated the goddess into their own mythology. The Greeks imagined the gods to be like humans. They even thought that gods regularly walked the Earth in human guise. The stories about these gods, which people told to each other, are called myths.

Aphrodite was one of these gods in human guise, and the successor to the goddess Astarte. According to the Greek author Homer, Aphrodite was the daughter of Zeus and Dione. She was born from the white foam of an ocean wave. She floated to Cyprus on a big shell, and set foot upon the island at Petra Tou Romiou. Homer was an important storyteller and poet who lived from 800 to about 750 BC. Little is known about him except that he was blind and was born on the Greek island of Chios. The *Iliad* and *Odyssey* are his most famous works.

▼ *This is the rock near the beach on which Aphrodite and her shell were washed ashore, according to the ancient Greek legend.*

▶ *The place where Aphrodite came ashore is called Petra Tou Romiou.*

In ancient times, people attributed events such as storms and earthquakes to the gods and goddesses because they could not explain them in any other way. These ancient peoples tried to appease the gods by making sacrifices to them. All kinds of products were sacrificed to the gods, including corn and oil. Often animals would be killed as a sacrifice, too. Sacrifices were also made to the gods for other reasons – for example when the ancient Greeks wanted a good harvest.

▲ *Remains at the Sanctuary of Aphrodite.*

There are many stories about Aphrodite. One of them takes place on Cyprus, and tells the tale of a king called Pygmalion. Pygmalion was very good at carving statues from ivory. Everyone loved his work. He once made a statue of a woman so beautiful that he fell in love with it. He called her Galatea. Every day, he could be found near the statue of Galatea. He would watch it for hours, and he would kiss the cold statue, hoping to 'thaw' her. One day, the limbs of the statue became soft and warm. The white lips of Galatea became red. The statue had come to life under his kisses. The goddess Aphrodite had felt compassion for the king, and had given life to the statue. The king and Galatea married, and had a son, Paphos, after whom the Cypriot city is named.

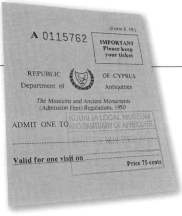

For this reason, the ancient people on Cyprus built many temples to worship Aphrodite and to male sacrifices to her. The most important site for her worshippers was the sanctuary near Paphos. Each year in April, when the trees and flowers were in full bloom, a festival would be held that lasted four days. Pilgrims from Greece and other countries would travel to Paphos and gather in a large square. From there, there was a big procession to the Sanctuary of Aphrodite. In exchange for a coin, each pilgrim would receive a handful of salt as a symbol of the fact that Aphrodite was born from the foam of a wave in the sea.

◀ ▼ *The Sanctuary of Aphrodite lies to the east of Paphos and was one of the most celebrated places of pilgrimage in ancient times. It dates from the twelfth century* BC.

Glossary

Bronze Age The period between around 2500 and 1050 BC, in which people made tools and weapons from the metal bronze

Byzantine Empire The eastern part of the Roman Empire after it split in AD 395.

Constitution A series of laws outlining the basic principles of a government or country.

Crusades A series of military campaigns in which knights from Christian states tried to 'free' other lands from Muslim occupation.

Knights Templar A group of knights who protected travellers who were on pilgrimages to the Holy Land.

Middle Ages The period from around AD 500 to 1450.

Orthodox Church The Christian Church in the East; it has several independent sects, including Greek Orthodox.

Roman Empire Established by Augustus in 27 BC to replace the Roman Republic. At its height the empire was the greatest in the world.

Stone Age The earliest period in technological history, when tools and weapons were made from stone.

United Nations An organization established in 1945, in which member nations work towards international peace and security.

Index

Eur

Iceland

The Countries of the European Union

Republic of Ireland	Portugal	Estonia	Finland	Austria
United Kingdom	Germany	Sweden	Greece	Latvia
Czech Republic	Denmark	Belgium	Poland	Spain
Luxembourg	Hungary	Slovakia	France	Italy
The Netherlands	Lithuania	Slovenia	Cyprus	Malta

NORTH SEA

Republic
of
Ireland

United Kingdom

The Nethe

Belgium

Luxembou

ATLANTIC OCEAN

France

Switzerland

Monaco

Portugal

Spain

MEDITERRANEAN

0		500 km
0		500 miles